Building
ON A
Dream

THE
GREAT
WALL
OF CHINA

Amie Jane Leavitt

PURPLE TOAD
PUBLISHING

PURPLE TOAD
PUBLISHING

Printing   1   2   3   4   5   6   7   8   9

BUILDING ON A DREAM

Big Ben
The Burj Khalifa
The Eiffel Tower
The Empire State Building
The Golden Gate Bridge
The Great Wall of China

The Leaning Tower of Pisa
The Space Needle
The Statue of Liberty
The Sydney Opera House
The Taj Mahal
The White House

Publisher's Cataloging-in-Publication Data
Leavitt, Amie Jane.
   The Great Wall of China/ written by Amie Jane Leavitt.
      p. cm.
Includes bibliographic references, glossary, and index.
ISBN 9781624693540
1. Great Wall of China (China)—Juvenile literature. 2. Architecture—Vocational guidance—Juvenile literature. I. Series: Building on a Dream: Kids as Architects and Engineers.
 NA2555 2017
 720
                                              Library of Congress Control Number: 2017940648
eBook ISBN: 9781624693557

ABOUT THE AUTHOR: Amie Jane Leavitt graduated from Brigham Young University and is an accomplished author, researcher, and photographer. She has written nearly a hundred books for kids and young adults, has contributed to online and print media, and has worked as a consultant, writer, and editor for numerous educational publishing and assessment companies. To check out a listing of Ms. Leavitt's current projects and published works, visit her website at www.amiejaneleavitt.com.

CONTENTS

MONGOLIA

MANCHURIA

INNER MONGOLIA

Jiayuguan Pass

Beijing

Shanhai Pass

Bo Hai Sea

CHINA

Tibetan Plateau

Tourists come from all over the world to walk along the top of the Great Wall. The map shows where parts of the Great Wall still stand—many centuries after they were built.

Dreaming of Security

A stone dragon twists and turns through the landscape of northern China. It follows mountain ridges. It descends down into valleys, crosses rivers, and sprawls through sandy deserts. On the eastern end, the dragon's head rests in the Yellow Sea. On the western end, the tail lies in the dusty mustard sand of the Gobi Desert. This stone dragon is the Great Wall of China.

Walls were an ancient security system in many countries. In China, every major city had a wall around it to keep out invaders. In fact, the Chinese word for "city" is the same word for "wall."[1] Walls were built around homes, too, for the same reasons. There's an old Chinese tradition that says that a house is not a house unless it has a wall around it.

Before the year 221 BCE, China was not a unified country. Instead, it was made up of several kingdoms. The kingdoms went to war against each other. They built walls around their borders to protect their lands and keep out the enemy.

That changed in 221 BCE. The kingdom of Qin (pronounced *chin*) had conquered all of the other kingdoms. For the first time in history, the area was under one leader, or emperor. The new emperor gave the unified country the name of China. He would be called Qin Shi Huang, or the First Emperor of China.[2]

One of Shi Huang's first orders of business was to take down the walls between the kingdoms. They were not necessary anymore since

Qin Shi Huang

the country was united. However, he decided that the few walls along the northern borders should be kept. He wanted to make them stronger and link them together. This would give the new kingdom a solid wall from one end to the other.

North of this wall lived the Mongols. This nomadic group of people would often come down into China and raid communities. They would steal food and harm the people in the villages. Shi Huang felt that the best way to stop these raids was to build a grand fortress for protection. He also dreamed that this wall would be a monument to himself as a great first leader of China.

Work began immediately on the emperor's wall. The people who worked on the wall did not do so because they wanted to. The emperor's generals forced them to work on the project. They were basically slaves, receiving little to no pay. Some had to travel thousands of miles from their homes to work on the wall.[3]

Some of the workers were the country's soldiers. Others were peasants who were forced into service. Convicts also worked on the wall. They had to wear certain clothing and chains to mark themselves as prisoners. The workers toiled in extreme heat during the summer and freezing conditions in the winter.

Around a million men helped build the wall. Approximately 400,000 of them died while working on it. Some were injured or killed on the job. Others died from exhaustion. The men got very little sleep, since they had to work so many hours each day. If they were caught napping on the job, punishment was often death. Some died because they did not have enough food to eat. Others died because of mistreatment by the bosses or because they got sick from diseases. When that many people live and work that close to one another, diseases can run rampant.[4]

Some of the men were hundreds or thousands of miles away from their homes. If they died on the job, their bodies could not be sent back to their families. Most were buried right where they died. It is believed that they were either buried in trenches along the wall or within the wall itself. Because of this, the Great Wall is also known as the longest cemetery in the world.[5]

Even though this wall was the dream of China's leader, it was definitely not a dream job. For the people who built it, it was a nightmare.

Thomas Allom, an English architect and artist, drew the Great Wall in 1845. His illustration captures the immense size of the wall.

In the rammed-earth technique, layers of soil and plant material were packed between wooden frames.

The First Wall

This first wall was not built using square-cut stone and perfectly formed bricks. Rather, workers used whatever material was near the construction site. If boulders and rocks happened to be nearby, they were pushed together to form part of the wall. But in many areas, another technique was used. It was called the rammed-earth construction process. In ancient times, it was common to use this process to build fences, defensive walls, and even walls for houses. It is still used sometimes when people want to build using a more natural method. In this process, the walls are made up of only soil, sand, and plants.[1]

To build a wall using the rammed-earth method, a frame is made out of timber. Two pieces of timber are placed on the ground parallel to each other, with space in between. The timber pieces are secured with wood braces to keep the frame from moving. Damp soil is shoveled into the frame. Then the workers use a long ramming pole called a tamper to pound the soil. This tool is simply a long stick tied to a flat or rounded surface. The surface is used to pound the soil.[2]

The workers would pound and pound the soil until it was hard and compacted. Then they would arrange a layer of reeds or grasses on top. Another thick layer of soil was added on top of the plants, and the workers would pound again. As the earthen wall grew higher, they would add more timber to make their frame taller. This kept all the compacted soil securely in place.[3]

Lines of workers would stand close together. Each one would tamp a small area.

The workers would repeat this process until the wall was the height they wanted. Once the wall was complete, the rammed earth would be as hard as stone. The reeds in the wall acted as a filtering system. When rainwater fell on the walls, it would seep down into the wall and then flow out of the wall at the reed layer.[4]

No one knows how long the Qin Dynasty wall was. Some think it was as long as 3,000 miles. That's about the distance from Boston to San Francisco. The walls were anywhere from 15 to 50 feet wide and were stacked some 15 to 30 feet high.

Some parts of the wall had additional structures built on top to protect the soldiers who guarded the wall. Those structures added another 12 feet to the height of the wall. Every so often, there were tall guard towers on the wall, too. Soldiers in these guard towers could watch for invaders.[5]

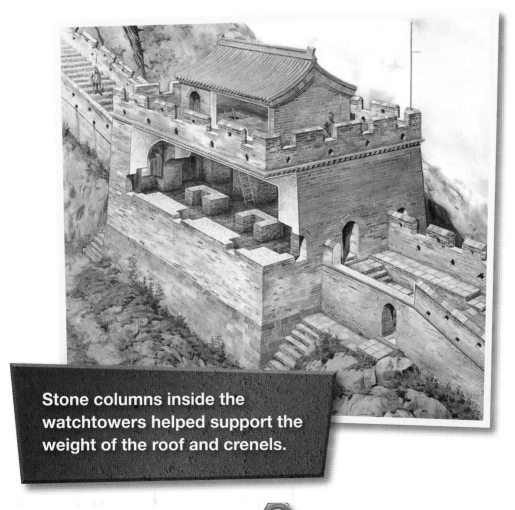

Stone columns inside the watchtowers helped support the weight of the roof and crenels.

Shi Huang was in power for only about 15 years. He spent 10 years of his reign building the wall. When he died, the Qin Dynasty eventually fell. It was replaced by the Han Dynasty, which reigned for about 400 years. During this time period, new sections of the wall were built, particularly in the desert area. They were also made with rammed earth. The soil in the desert is different from the soil in other areas. It is sandy and often contains tiny bits of shells. The shells are helpful in the rammed-earth technique. They are made up of a compound called calcium carbonate. When this material is exposed to water, it turns to a rock-solid material similar to cement.[6]

The remains of a Han era wall reveal the white shell pieces that were used to strengthen the wall.

A watchtower made using the rammed-earth technique during the Han Dynasty. It is slowly crumbling back into the desert.

The rammed-earth technique was a good way to make these early walls. Invaders would have been equipped with very simple weapons, such as swords, spears, and bows and arrows. These weapons would not have been able to break through the wall. However, once gunpowder was invented and people began using cannons and guns, the rammed-earth wall needed to be replaced with something sturdier.[7]

An ancient kiln, abandoned when it was time to move to the next section of the wall. Bricks were fired in these extremely hot ovens.

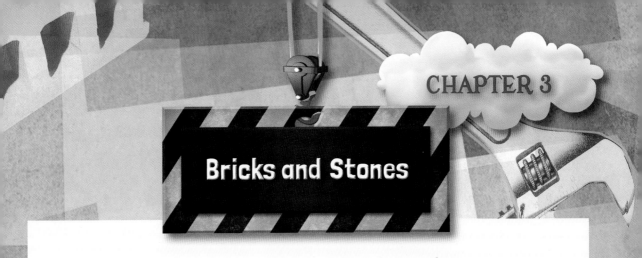

Bricks and Stones

Today's Great Wall of China, with its brick and stone fortresses, was built during the Ming Dynasty, from 1474 to 1644. Engineers and skilled tradesmen such as masons and stonecutters worked on the project.[1]

To make the bricks, special factories were built as close to the wall as possible. When work reached the mountain ridges, the factories were set up at the base of those mountains. The bricks were then hauled up to the worksite by humans or animals. Other basic equipment was used as well, including handcarts and wagons.

Bricks are formed out of raw materials, such as clay, sand, and water, all mixed together. The mixture would be thick, like cookie dough. Brick makers pressed the mixture into rectangular wooden frames. They wiped the top to make it smooth. Then they removed the frame and placed the wet brick somewhere to dry. In poor weather, a special drying building was used. In sunny weather, the bricks were placed in the sun.

Once they were nearly dry, the bricks were put into a kiln. In this hot oven, they would be exposed to low temperatures at first. This would complete the drying process. Then the temperature would be increased to a blazing 1,500 to 2,000 degrees Fahrenheit. This final firing step turned the brick into a block as hard as stone.

Bricks can be made into any size. The bricks used in the Great Wall weighed about 22 pounds each. They were about 15 inches long, 4 inches tall, and 7 inches deep.[2]

Besides bricks, stones were also used in the Ming Wall. Granite and limestone, including marble, were often used. The type of stone depended upon what was available in the mountains near the building site. Stone was mainly used for the foundation of the wall and for the tall towers. Huge slabs of stone were chiseled, hammered, and cut out of quarries. Then they were hauled up the mountainside to the wall. This was a lot more challenging than hauling the bricks because the stones were much larger and heavier. Once the stones were brought to the wall, they were lifted into place using such simple machines as ropes and pulleys.

The stones and the bricks were pasted together with mortar. Today, mortar is made out of lime, cement, and sand, all mixed with water. It is about as thick as cake frosting. For the Great Wall, the mortar was made of powdered limestone and an unusual ingredient: sticky rice! Mixed together, these two things made a very strong mortar that even plants could not grow through.[3]

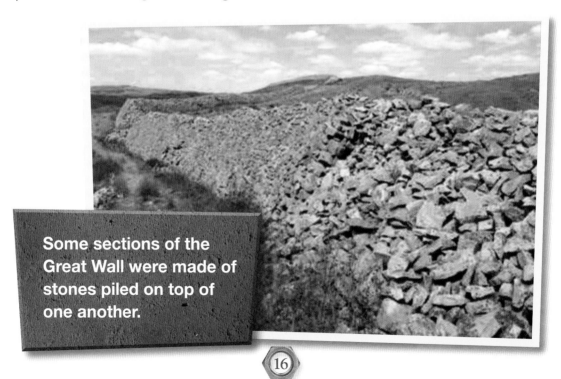

Some sections of the Great Wall were made of stones piled on top of one another.

Millions of people worked on the Ming Wall. They were brought in from all over the country. Just as with the Qin Wall, the conditions were rough. The work was hard, exhausting, and dangerous. In fact, since the men were working with heavy items like bricks and stones, the work was even more dangerous on the Ming Wall. Many thousands of men died on the job, just as they did on the Qin Wall.

The Ming Wall construction went on for nearly two hundred years. During that time, communities settled along the wall. The families of the workers built villages so that they could see their loved ones more often. Many of the people who live in these villages today are descendants of these Ming Wall workers.[4]

People enjoy hiking the Great Wall in 1907.

Juyongguan Pass. Some of the passes have been restored and painted in bright colors.

Ming Wall Design

The Ming Wall was more than just a wall. It also had signal towers and passes. The walls were built between the signal towers and passes to connect them.

Signal towers were spaced every couple hundred yards. Tower foundations were usually square or rectangular. They were about 20 feet wide. The roof was about 16 feet across. The height of the tower was anywhere between 16 and 26 feet. On top of the tower was an enclosed structure in which soldiers who guarded the wall could live. Outside the enclosure was an open area, where the soldiers could build signal fires. If an enemy was approaching, the soldiers in the watchtower would light a bonfire. When the guards in the adjacent towers saw the fire, they would light their own fires. This would continue from one end of the wall to the other. This allowed signals to be sent very quickly across vast distances. When the wall was finished, it had more than 25,000 watchtowers.[1]

The passes were areas where people could pass through the wall. They were often located where the wall crossed major trade routes or highways. Passes were also at the entrances to cities like Beijing. They were closely guarded to keep out invaders. Not everyone who approached them would be allowed through.

The passes weren't just a gap with a gate. Rather, they were a complete fortress. The base of the fortress was either a square or polygon. The walls of the passes were 33 feet high and contained

primary and secondary walls. They were wide enough for four horses to walk shoulder to shoulder along the top.[2]

In the center of the walled pass was a tall gate tower, which was two or three stories high. These were built to look like pagodas and were brightly painted. They served as guard towers.

Around the base of the fortress was a moat. This deep trench was filled with water and served as another form of defense. A bridge would be lowered or raised over the moat to either allow or prevent people from crossing the water. People had to pass through several gates in order to get to the other side of the fortress. Some of these gates were made of wood, and others were made of iron. Ramps and stairs led to the gates. Ramps could be used by horses and other animals.[3]

Some of the passes were simple, with just a few extra walls and gates. However, some passes were more like castles. The most famous castle-like passes are found at Shanhaiguan, Huangyaguan, Jiayuguan, and Juyongguan. The Juyongguan pass is the largest and most elaborate. It guarded the city of Beijing.

The walls connected the passes and signal towers. They are about 25 feet wide at the bottom, 16 feet wide at the top, and rise about 24 feet high. The walls

This Ming Dynasty fortress is located at Shanhaiguan, about 190 miles from Beijing.

are wide enough for either ten men or five horses to walk side by side. It is estimated that the Ming Wall is about 5,500 miles long. There are both inner and outer walls that run parallel to each other.[4]

The walls were built with two sides of brick or stone, and then filled in with soil, gravel, and pebbles. On top of the fill, more stones and bricks were placed to create a wide sidewalk or roadway. Along the top of the walls, there are specific designs that serve several purposes. The parapets or battlements are about six feet high. They

Crenels are cutouts in the wall that allowed soldiers to fight the enemy on the other side.

prevent people who are walking on the wall from falling off. They also protect people on the wall during an enemy attack. Regularly spaced cutouts called crenels are like windows. Soldiers can crouch behind them while shooting at the enemy. Cannons could be set up behind the crenels, too. The crenels give the top of the wall its distinctive boxed shape.

There are also small holes in the walls, used for drainage. When rain would fall, the top of the wall would be flooded unless there was some way to drain the water. To address this issue, drainage systems were built along the upper pathways. They are similar to the gutters along sidewalks today. On the wall, the water flows into these gutters and then out through the drainage holes.

The Mutianyu section of the wall was built during the Ming era. It has been fully restored.

The Wall Today

A lot of mystery and mythology surround the Great Wall. There is so much about this structure that is still to be discovered. However, based on what is known about the wall, many of these myths can be proven untrue.

Some people think the wall is one long structure that stretches from one part of China to another. In reality, there are many different sections of the wall. Some are not connected to each other at all. Some run parallel to each other and form a network of defenses. Some are found as far north and east as Russia and North Korea. Some of the wall's sections are so remote that people are still discovering them. The Ming Wall, which is the image of the Great Wall today, stretches about 5,500 miles. Experts believe that if you add the length of the Ming Wall to all the walls from other dynasties, the total length would be about 13,000 miles. That is more than halfway around the equator. This is indeed the longest manmade structure that has ever been built.[1]

Second, people think the Great Wall was built all at the same time. In fact, it was built by many different groups of people over 2,000 years. The wall we think of today as the Great Wall, the brick and stone structure, was built during the Ming Dynasty over a nearly 200-year time span.[2]

Third, some people think that the entire Great Wall is built out of bricks and stones with soaring watchtowers. It isn't. The area of the wall that is closest to Beijing looks like this. That's the part of the wall that most people visit, so it is natural that people would think the entire wall

This western section of the wall features rammed-earth, not bricks and stones.

looks like this. Other parts of the wall, though, are actually made up of other types of building materials. For example, in the desert areas of China, the wall is essentially just packed earth.[3]

Fourth, many people believe that you can see the Great Wall from the moon and from outer space. NASA astronauts say this is a common question. The astronauts who visited the moon confirmed that the Great Wall could not be seen from this distance. The only time the Great Wall has been viewed from space is from satellites that circle in Low-Earth Orbit.[4]

One thing is definitely true about the Great Wall. It is a grand landmark that needs to be taken care of and protected. Erosion continually breaks down sections of the wall. Scientists monitor this landmark to see what they can do to prevent further damage.

Humans also cause damage to the Great Wall. During the Communist Cultural Revolution (1966–1976), sections of the wall were completely torn down. Highways were built through some of those areas. The brick and stone were used to construct nearby apartment buildings.[5]

In the past, villagers would chisel out pieces of the wall, and then sell them to tourists as souvenirs. This practice is very much discouraged today.

Restoration on the wall by the Chinese Government has been ongoing since the 1980s. At that time, the wall nearest Beijing was repaired and restored. In certain areas today, the Great Wall is crumbling due to both erosion and human influences. Some people still try to take parts of the wall for souvenirs or for building supplies. The Chinese government is doing its best to stop destruction on the wall by these influences.[6]

The Great Wall is one of the most widely recognized symbols of China. Thousands of people visit it every day. In fact, it is one of the most visited attractions in the world. When many people think of China, they picture the Great Wall snaking across green mountain ranges. Many people who visit the country do not want to leave before they walk atop the stone pathway of the Great Wall.

Maybe one day, you'll get to walk along the back of the stone dragon too!

The Great Wall snakes across the mountaintops in China.

About 400 BCE   Separate kingdoms in China build walls on their borders as protection from one another.

221 BCE   First emperor of a united China is Qin Dynasty's ruler Qin Shi Huang. He orders the construction of a northern border wall. When finished, it is believed to stretch about 3,000 miles.

207 BCE   Qin Shi Huang dies. The Qin Dynasty falls.

206 BCE–220 CE   Han Dynasty continues to build the wall.

220 CE   Frontier tribes seize control of northern China.

386–535   Northern Wei Dynasty repairs and extends the wall to defend against attacks.

550–577   Bei Qi kingdom builds and repairs more than 900 miles of the wall.

581–618   Sui Dynasty repairs and extends the wall several times.

618–907   During the Tang Dynasty, China controls land on both sides of the wall. The Great Wall loses its importance as a fortification.

906–1279   During the Song Dynasty, the Chinese are pushed back to their original side of the wall.

1206–1368   Mongol leader Genghis Khan eventually takes over all of China and establishes the Yuan Dynasty. Soldiers are stationed on the Great Wall to protect the people and goods that pass through on the trade route.

1368	Ming Dynasty comes to power. Early leaders have little interest in building border walls.
1421	Beijing is named the new capital of China. Chinese culture flourishes.
1474	Construction on the Great Wall begins. The wall stretches from Juyong Pass (near the Yellow River) in the west to the Yellow Sea in the east.
1570	The Great Wall is costing more than three-fourths of the government's income.
1644	Ming Dynasty falls. Construction on the wall ends.
1700s–1800s	The Great Wall becomes the most common symbol of China for countries in the West.
1960s	The Chinese government dismantles parts of the Great Wall during the Cultural Revolution. Stones and bricks are used for other building projects.
1980s	The Chinese communist government tries to restore the damage to the Great Wall, especially the area closest to Beijing.
2017	In certain areas, the Great Wall crumbles due to natural forces (erosion) and human influence (souvenir collecting). The Chinese government tries to repair some areas but ends up causing additional damage to the landmark.

Chapter 1
1. "Modern Marvels: Great Wall of China," History Channel, Youtube.
2. Ibid.
3. "Building the Great Wall," History.com video.
4. "Great Wall of China," History.com
5. "Building the Great Wall," History.com video.

Chapter 2
1. "The Original Great Wall," Science Channel, Unearthed Videos.
2. Ibid.
3. "Great Wall of China," History.com
4. Ibid.
5. "Building the Great Wall," History.com video.
6. "The Original Great Wall," Science Channel, Unearthed Videos.
7. "Great Wall Construction Material," Travel China Guide.

Chapter 3
1. "Building the Great Wall," History.com video.
2. "Great Wall of China," National Geographic video.
3. "Great Wall of China: Strength Comes From Sticky Rice," Telegraph.co.uk
4. "Behind the Great Wall," Discovery Channel Documentary, video.

Chapter 4
1. "Great Wall of China," National Geographic video.
2. "Modern Marvels: Great Wall of China," History Channel, Youtube.
3. "Building the Great Wall," History.com video.
4. "Great Wall of China," Engineering.com

Chapter 5
1. "Great Wall of China," National Geographic video.
2. Ibid.
3. "Building the Great Wall," History.com video.
4. Ibid.
5. "Modern Marvels: Great Wall of China," History Channel, Youtube.
6. John F. Burns, "Restoring the Great Wall."

Books

Demuth, Patricia Brennan. *Where Is the Great Wall?* New York: Grosset & Dunlap, 2015.

Jones, Cathy. *Discovery Kids: Wonders of the World.* Bath, UK: Parragon Books, 2016.

Mann, Elizabeth. *The Great Wall: The Story of Thousands of Miles of Earth and Stone That Turned a Nation into a Fortress.* New York: Mikaya Press, 2011.

Morley, Jacqueline, and David Salariya. *You Wouldn't Want to Work on the Great Wall of China!: Defenses You'd Rather Not Build.* New York: Franklin Watts, 2011.

Stanborough, Rebecca. *The Great Wall of China* (Engineering Wonders). Mankato, MN: Capstone Press, 2016.

Yamashita, Michael. *The Great Wall: From Beginning to End.* New York: Sterling Publishing, 2011.

On the Internet

History Channel: Great Wall of China
http://www.history.com/topics/great-wall-of-china

National Geographic: Great Wall of China
http://www.nationalgeographic.com/travel/world-heritage/great-wall-china/

Science Kids: Engineering Facts, Great Wall of China
http://www.sciencekids.co.nz/sciencefacts/engineering/greatwallofchina.html

UNESCO: The Great Wall
http://whc.unesco.org/en/list/438

USA Today: Facts about the Great Wall of China for Kids
http://traveltips.usatoday.com/great-wall-china-kids-61571.html

Works Consulted

"Behind the Great Wall." Discovery Channel Documentary. YouTube (Video). Published December 9, 2012. https://www.youtube.com/watch?v=yRKS2b3Ugz8

"Builders of the Great Wall." History.com (Video). http://www.history.com/topics/great-wall-of-china/videos/seven-wonders-the-great-wall?m=528e394da93ae&s=undefined&f=1&free=false

"Building the Great Wall." History.com (Video). http://www.history.com/topics/great-wall-of-china/videos/building-the-great-wall

Burns, John F. "Restoring the Great Wall." *New York Times*, September 8, 1985. http://www.nytimes.com/1985/09/08/travel/restoring-the-great-wall-of-china.html?pagewanted=all

Cliff, Betsy D. "On the Wall." *Dartmouth Magazine,* December 2010. http://dartmouthalumnimagazine.com/articles/wall

"Great Wall of China." Engineering.com, October 17, 2006. http://www.engineering.com/DesignerEdge/DesignerEdgeArticles/ArticleID/80/The-Great-Wall-of-China.aspx

"Great Wall of China." National Geographic (Video). http://video.nationalgeographic.com/video/exploreorg/china-great-wall-eorg

"Modern Marvels: Great Wall of China." History Channel. YouTube (Video). January 15, 2017. (https://www.youtube.com/watch?v=Yw792VTbNJc).

"National Geographic Great Wall of China." YouTube (Video). December 13, 2012. https://www.youtube.com/watch?v=RyHJCWfQYwo

Unveiling the Great Wall of China. Dream Big Film. http://www.dreambigfilm.com/stories/unveiling-the-great-wall-of-china/

adjacent (ud-JAY-sent)—Next to.

ancient (AYN-chent)—Occurring a very long time ago.

battlement (BAT-ul-ment)—A wall on the top of a wall or castle with cutouts (crenels) that can be used for shooting. Also known as a parapet.

compact (kom-PAKT)—To push down, compress, or make dense.

convict (KON-vikt)—A person who has been found guilty (convicted) of a crime and is serving prison time.

crenel (KREN-ul)—A cutout in a wall that can be used as a window for shooting or firing cannons.

emperor (EM-per-er)—A king or monarch.

erosion (ee-ROH-zhun)—The wearing down of rock and stone by natural forces, including water, wind, and chemicals.

fortress (FOR-trus)—A structure that is built for security and protection.

foundation (fown-DAY-shun)—The part of a building that is connected to the ground and is made of strong materials that can support whatever is built on it.

kiln (KILN)—An oven for baking clay objects.

marble (MAR-bul)—Limestone that has crystallized.

mason (MAY-sun)—A person who works with stone.

moat (MOHT)—A ditch with water in it. These are often found around castles.

monument (MAHN-yoo-munt)—A statue, building, or other structure that is meant to honor a particular person or group of people.

mortar (MOR-tur)—A special paste that fastens tile, bricks, and stone together.

nomadic (noh-MAD-ik)—A lifestyle where groups of people travel from place to place and do not have a settled home.

pagoda (puh-GOH-dah)—A Buddhist temple; a common architectural style throughout Asia.

parapet (PAYR-uh-pet)—See *battlement*.

polygon (PAH-lee-gon)—A closed shape with many straight sides. The prefix *poly* means "many."

quarry (KWOR-ee)—A place where stone is cut from the earth for use in buildings and other structures.

timber (TIM-ber)—Wood.

tradition (truh-DIH-shun)—A set of beliefs, ideas, or ways of doing things that is passed on from one generation to another.

trench (TRENTCH)—A long ditch.

PHOTO CREDITS: p. I—Nomad Foto; p. 4—Peter Dowley; p. 13—Real Bear; p. 20—NH53; p. 22—Lydia Liu; p. 24—Dan Lundberg; p. 25—LW Yang. All other photos—Public Domain. Every measure has been taken to find all copyright holders of material used in this book. In the event any mistakes or omissions have happened within, attempts to correct them will be made in future editions of the book.